CATALONIA Guide 2025

Uncovering the Essence of Spain's Art, Nature, and Culinary Delights"

By

Ruth W. Scott

Copyright @ Ruth W. Scott, 2025

All Rights Reserved. Except for brief quotations included in critical reviews and certain other noncommercial uses permitted by copyright law, no part of this publication may be reproduced, distributed, or transmitted in any form or by any means, including photocopying, recording, or other electronic or mechanical methods

DISCLAIMER

This guide to Catalonia aims to offer helpful information and recommendations for your trip. While we've taken care to ensure accuracy at the time of writing, details such as prices, schedules, and regulations may change.

We encourage travelers to confirm specifics with relevant authorities, businesses, or service providers. The authors and publishers are not responsible for any losses, inconveniences, or issues arising from the use of this guide.

Please travel responsibly, respecting local laws, customs, and environmental practices.

ACKNOWLEDGEMENT

This guidebook owes its creation to the support and contributions of many individuals and organizations. We are deeply grateful to the people of Catalonia, locals, historians, and tourism experts, who shared their knowledge, stories, and expertise.

Our appreciation also goes to the businesses, cultural institutions, and community leaders who provided invaluable assistance. To travelers whose passion for exploration inspires guides like this, thank you for your curiosity and enthusiasm.

Lastly, we celebrate the remarkable history, culture, and natural beauty of Catalonia, which makes it a truly extraordinary destination. Thank you for letting us share its wonders.

TABLE OF CONTENTS

INTRODUCTION TO CATALONIA
- Welcome to Catalonia
- Geography, Climate, and Key Facts
- Catalonia's Unique Identity: Language, Culture, and Traditions

CHAPTER 1: PLANNING YOUR TRIP
- Best Times to Visit
- Entry Points: Airports, Trains, and Roads
- Navigating Catalonia: Transportation Options
- Budgeting Your Trip

CHAPTER 2: BARCELONA – THE CAPITAL OF CATALONIA
- Top Landmarks: Sagrada Família, Park Güell, and Gothic Quarter
- Art and Architecture: Gaudí and Beyond
- Exploring Neighborhoods: El Born, Eixample, and Gràcia
- Beaches, Markets, and Nightlife

CHAPTER 3: THE COSTA BRAVA
- Best Beaches and Seaside Towns
- The Dalí Triangle: Figueres, Cadaqués, and Púbol
- Outdoor Adventures: Snorkeling, Diving, and Coastal Walks
- Hidden Villages and Scenic Drives

CHAPTER 4: THE PYRENEES AND RURAL ESCAPES
- Hiking, Skiing, and Adventure Sports

    Picturesque Villages: Vall de Núria, Rupit, and Besalú
    National Parks and Wildlife Reserves
    Cultural Highlights in the Mountains

CHAPTER 5: HISTORIC CITIES – GIRONA AND TARRAGONA
    Girona: Medieval Streets and Modern Charm
    The Cathedral, Jewish Quarter, and River Onyar
    Tarragona: Roman Heritage on the Coast
    Amphitheater, Forum, and UNESCO Sites
    Local Cuisine and Historical Tours

CHAPTER 6: CATALAN CUISINE AND GASTRONOMY
    Traditional Dishes: Pa amb Tomàquet, Escudella, and Crema Catalana
    Wine Regions: Penedès, Priorat, and Empordà
    Cava Tasting: The Sparkling Wine of Catalonia
    Markets, Tapas Bars, and Michelin-Starred Restaurants

CHAPTER 7: FESTIVALS AND CULTURAL TRADITIONS
    Iconic Events: La Mercè, Castells, and Sant Jordi
    Folklore, Music, and Dance
    Local Celebrations and Seasonal Festivals
    Experiencing Catalonia's Vibrant Community Spirit

CHAPTER 8: OUTDOOR ADVENTURES AND NATURAL WONDERS
    Montserrat: The Iconic Mountain and Monastery
    National and Natural Parks: Aiguamolls de l'Empordà, Montseny, and Garrotxa
    Scenic Routes: Coastal Walks and Biking Trails

- Eco-Tourism and Wildlife

CHAPTER 9: FAMILY-FRIENDLY CATALONIA
- Theme Parks: PortAventura and Tibidabo
- Kid-Friendly Beaches and Outdoor Activities
- Interactive Museums and Cultural Experiences for All Ages
- Planning a Memorable Family Trip

CHAPTER 10: PRACTICAL INFORMATION AND TRAVEL TIPS
- Accommodation: Hotels, Villas, and Rural Retreats
- Language, Currency, and Etiquette
- Safety, Health, and Emergency Contacts
- Sustainability and Responsible Tourism
- Maps and navigation tools

CHAPTER 11: SUGGESTED ITINERARIES
- 7-Day Journey: Coastal, Cultural, and Rural Explorations
- Thematic Routes: Wine, History, and Nature
- Day Trips: Montserrat, Andorra, and the French Pyrenees

CONCLUSION

INTRODUCTION TO CATALONIA

Welcome to Catalonia

Stretching from the peaks of the Pyrenees to the shores of the Mediterranean, Catalonia is a region brimming with culture, history, and breathtaking scenery. From the vibrant energy of Barcelona to the golden beaches of the Costa Brava and the medieval allure of Girona, there's something here for every kind of traveler.

Whether you're drawn to its stunning architecture, famous culinary scene, or diverse natural landscapes, Catalonia offers experiences that will stay with you long after your visit. Immerse yourself in its lively festivals, rich traditions, and welcoming spirit.

Geography, Climate, and Key Facts

Nestled in northeastern Spain, Catalonia boasts a stunningly diverse landscape. Covering around 32,000 square kilometers, it stretches from the majestic Pyrenees Mountains in the north to the idyllic Mediterranean coastline in the east. Its varied geography includes golden beaches, lush vineyards, rugged peaks, and scenic woodlands. The region is divided into four provinces: Barcelona, Girona, Lleida, and Tarragona, each with its own unique charm.

Climate

Catalonia experiences a predominantly Mediterranean climate, with hot, dry summers and mild, wetter winters along the coast. Inland areas, particularly near the Pyrenees, have a more continental climate with colder winters and occasional snowfall. Spring and autumn offer mild, pleasant weather, making them ideal seasons for outdoor activities and sightseeing.

Key Facts

Capital: Barcelona, a vibrant center of art, architecture, and gastronomy.

Population: Approximately 7.7 million.

Languages: Catalan and Spanish are both official languages.

Currency: Euro (€).

Highlights: Iconic landmarks like Sagrada Família, Park Güell, the Costa Brava, Montserrat, and the Dalí Theatre-Museum.

Cultural Identity: Catalonia is known for its rich traditions, such as castells (human towers), Correfoc fire festivals, and its modernist architectural treasures recognized by UNESCO.

With its varied terrain, pleasant weather, and vibrant culture, Catalonia is a destination that offers endless possibilities for exploration and discovery.

Catalonia's Unique Identity: Language, Culture, and Traditions

Catalonia's identity is firmly rooted in its distinct language, culture, and customs, which distinguish it from the rest of Spain. With a long history of seeking autonomy, the region takes immense pride in its heritage, which is evident in its festivals, daily life, and artistic expressions.

Language

Catalan is central to Catalonia's identity. Spoken alongside Spanish, it is the official language in both regional institutions and daily activities. It is used widely in schools, media, and public life, embodying the region's strong sense of cultural individuality.

Culture

Catalonia is home to a dynamic cultural scene that blends traditional influences with modern creativity. The works of famous artists like Antoni Gaudí and Salvador Dalí, as well as its iconic architecture, such as the modernist buildings in Barcelona, define the region's artistic legacy. Catalan cuisine also reflects its unique culture, with signature dishes such as pa amb tomàquet (bread with tomato), calçots (grilled spring onions), and crema catalana (a custard dessert).

Traditions

The region's rich traditions are an integral part of Catalan life. Celebrations like the Castells (human towers) and Correfoc (fire festivals) highlight the community's creativity and unity. The Sardana dance, performed in public spaces, and the Diada de Catalunya (Catalan National Day) on September 11th, are expressions of the region's historical pride and dedication to preserving its culture.

Catalonia's distinct blend of language, culture, and traditions makes it an exceptional destination where visitors can truly experience its unique identity.

CHAPTER 1: PLANNING YOUR TRIP

Best Times to Visit

Catalonia is a fantastic destination throughout the year, with the best time to visit depending on your preferred weather, crowd levels, and activities. Here's a guide to the top seasons:

Spring (March to May)
Spring offers pleasant temperatures and fewer tourists, making it one of the most enjoyable times to visit. Nature blooms, and it's a great time for outdoor pursuits like hiking in the Pyrenees or leisurely walks through Barcelona's parks.

Summer (June to August)
Summer brings hot, sunny weather, perfect for enjoying the Mediterranean beaches of Costa Brava and Costa Daurada. However, this is also peak tourist season, so expect larger crowds. Summer is ideal for beachgoers and festival enthusiasts, with events like La Patum de Berga and Festa Major de Gracia taking place.

Autumn (September to November)

Autumn is another excellent time to visit, with warm temperatures in September and October and fewer tourists than summer. It's perfect for exploring cities like Barcelona and Girona, as well as experiencing the harvest season in the vineyards. The fall foliage in the Pyrenees also adds to the region's charm.

Winter (December to February)

Winter in Catalonia is generally mild, though colder in the mountains. For winter sports enthusiasts, the Pyrenees offer skiing and snowboarding opportunities. The holiday season also brings festive markets and local celebrations, offering a cozy, atmospheric experience.

In summary, spring and autumn offer mild weather and fewer crowds, while summer is best for beach activities and festivals, and winter is ideal for skiing or enjoying the festive charm of the season.

Entry Points: Airports, Trains, and Roads

Catalonia is well-connected, offering various entry points to suit different travel preferences. Whether arriving by air, rail, or road, the region is easily accessible.

Airports

The primary gateway to Catalonia is Barcelona-El Prat Airport (BCN), located just 12 km from Barcelona's city center. It is the busiest airport in the region, offering flights to numerous international destinations. Other key airports include Girona-Costa Brava Airport (GRO), which is popular with budget airlines, and Reus Airport (REU), mainly serving the Tarragona area and Costa Daurada.

Trains

Catalonia has an extensive and efficient train network, making it easy to travel around the region. Barcelona Sants Station is the main railway hub, with high-speed AVE trains connecting Barcelona to Madrid and other major cities in Spain. Local trains (Rodalies) provide access to surrounding areas, while RENFE trains link cities like Girona, Tarragona, and Lleida. The Catalan Railways (FGC) network serves the Pyrenees and mountainous areas.

Roads

The region also offers a well-developed network of highways and roads, ideal for those traveling by car. The AP-7 highway connects Barcelona to the French border and runs along the Costa Brava. The A-2 and C-16 highways link to inland cities like Lleida and Andorra. Renting a car is a great option for exploring rural areas or destinations that are off the beaten path.

Whether arriving by plane, train, or car, Catalonia provides plenty of convenient options to begin your adventure and explore its diverse attractions.

Navigating Catalonia: Transportation Options

Getting around Catalonia is straightforward, with a variety of transportation options that make it easy to explore both the cities and the countryside.

Public Transport

Catalonia's public transportation system is efficient and well-connected, particularly in cities like Barcelona. The Barcelona Metro is an extensive subway network, perfect for traveling quickly around the city and its surrounding areas. The bus network covers the entire region, providing convenient options for both short and longer journeys. Trams also offer easy access to key parts of Barcelona. For regional travel, Rodalies and Catalan Railways (FGC) connect towns and the Pyrenees.

Taxis and Ride-Sharing

Taxis are readily available throughout Catalonia, and ride-sharing services like Uber and Cabify are also operational, offering a flexible way to get around, especially for shorter trips or when public transport is not an option.

Car Rentals

Renting a car is a great choice for those wanting to explore more remote areas of Catalonia. With well-maintained highways such as the AP-7 and A-2, it's easy to drive between cities, coastal towns, and the mountains. Car rental services are available at airports and major train stations.

Biking

Cycling is a fantastic way to explore Catalonia, particularly in cities like Barcelona, which boasts extensive bike lanes and bike-sharing schemes. The region's coastal routes and mountain paths also offer scenic cycling opportunities for those who enjoy a slower pace.

Ferries

For those looking to explore Catalonia's coastal areas or travel to the Balearic Islands, ferries provide a convenient and scenic travel option. Regular ferry routes run from Barcelona to popular destinations like Mallorca and Ibiza.

With options ranging from metros to taxis, trains to bikes, and even ferries, Catalonia makes it easy to explore every corner of the region.

Budgeting Your Trip

Catalonia offers a wide range of options for travelers, whether you're on a tight budget or looking for a more luxurious experience. Planning your expenses in advance will help you get the most out of your trip.

Accommodation

Accommodation in Catalonia caters to all budgets. In cities like Barcelona, you'll find everything from budget-friendly hostels to mid-range hotels and high-end resorts. For a more economical stay, consider looking in smaller towns or rural areas, where guesthouses and Airbnb rentals are typically cheaper. Booking early can also help you secure better deals.

Dining

Catalonia offers a diverse food scene, with options ranging from casual tapas bars and local cafés to fine dining. To save money, try the menu del día (set-menu lunch) at local eateries, which is often a more affordable way to dine. Street food, such as those found at La Boqueria market in Barcelona, offers fresh and tasty options at lower prices.

Transportation

Public transport in Catalonia is convenient and inexpensive. The Barcelona Metro and buses offer travel passes, like the T10 ticket (10 trips), which can save you money. If you plan to travel between cities, keep an eye out for discounted train tickets or bus offers. Renting a car is also an option, but remember that expenses like fuel, tolls, and parking can add up.

Attractions

Many of Catalonia's attractions, such as parks, beaches, and hiking trails, are free or low-cost. However, popular sites like Sagrada Família and the Picasso Museum charge an entry fee. To save, consider purchasing a Barcelona Pass or similar city passes, which offer discounted entry to various attractions and include public transport.

Shopping and Souvenirs

Catalonia's markets are a great way to experience local culture. Browsing places like La Boqueria or Mercat de Sant Antoni can be done without spending much. For souvenirs, consider picking up local products like wine, olive oil, or handmade crafts, which are often more affordable than typical tourist items.

By managing your budget for accommodation, meals, transport, and activities, you can enjoy all that Catalonia has to offer without overspending. Whether you're on a budget or ready to indulge, the region offers options to fit all financial preferences.

CHAPTER 2: BARCELONA – THE CAPITAL OF CATALONIA

Top Landmarks: Sagrada Família, Park Güell, and Gothic Quarter

Catalonia boasts numerous iconic landmarks, with Barcelona being home to some of its most celebrated attractions. Among the must-see sites are Sagrada Família, Park Güell, and the Gothic Quarter.

Sagrada Família

A world-renowned symbol of Barcelona, the Sagrada Família is Antoni Gaudí's masterpiece. This extraordinary basilica, still under construction after over a century, is famous for its unique, nature-inspired architecture. Its elaborate facades, stunning interiors, and towering spires leave visitors in awe, making it a must-visit for any traveler.

Park Güell

Designed by Gaudí, Park Güell is a whimsical public park that seamlessly blends artistic design with nature. With its colorful mosaics, distinctive sculptures, and sweeping views of the city, it's a great place to relax and explore. The park's iconic dragon statue, adorned in bright tiles, is a favorite photo spot.

Gothic Quarter

The Gothic Quarter is Barcelona's historic center, known for its maze-like streets, medieval buildings, and hidden squares. Visitors can wander through landmarks like the Barcelona Cathedral, visit Plaça Sant Jaume, and discover traces of the city's Roman history. The quarter's charming atmosphere and historical significance make it a must-see for anyone wanting to experience Barcelona's rich cultural heritage.

These landmarks offer just a taste of the architectural beauty and historical depth that Catalonia has to offer. From Gaudí's masterpieces to the historic streets of the Gothic Quarter, these iconic sites are essential highlights of any visit to the region.

Art and Architecture: Gaudí and Beyond

Catalonia is a region where art and architecture come together in spectacular ways, particularly through the genius of Antoni Gaudí, whose work has left an indelible mark on Barcelona and beyond. However, Catalonia's artistic heritage extends far beyond Gaudí, offering a diverse range of architectural styles and artistic movements.

Gaudí's Masterpieces

Gaudí's influence on Catalonian architecture is undeniable. His works, including the Sagrada Família, Park Güell, and Casa Batlló, showcase his distinct approach to design, blending organic forms with vibrant colors and innovative structures. Gaudí's ability to integrate nature into his architecture makes his work stand out as both visionary and timeless. His creations remain some of the most visited and admired landmarks in the world.

Modernisme and the Catalan Art Nouveau Movement

While Gaudí is the most famous figure, the Modernisme movement (Catalan Art Nouveau) has shaped much of Barcelona's architectural landscape. Architects like Lluís Domènech i Montaner and Josep Puig i Cadafalch contributed to the movement with buildings like Palau de la Música Catalana and Casa Amatller, respectively. These structures are characterized by ornate facades, decorative tiles, and a fusion of traditional Catalan elements with modern designs.

Gothic Architecture and Beyond

Catalonia is also home to a rich history of Gothic architecture, particularly evident in the Gothic Quarter of Barcelona. The Barcelona Cathedral and Santa Maria del Mar are prime examples of the grandeur and intricacy of the Gothic style, with soaring spires, ribbed vaults, and stunning stained-glass windows. The influence of earlier periods, including Romanesque and Renaissance, can also be seen in Catalonia's churches, monasteries, and palaces.

Contemporary Art and Architecture

In addition to historical styles, Catalonia embraces contemporary architecture and art. Barcelona's Museu d'Art Contemporani de Barcelona (MACBA) and Fundació Joan Miró are testaments to the region's commitment to modern art. Architects like Ricardo Bofill and Jean Nouvel have designed cutting-edge structures that blend innovation with Catalan tradition. The Torre Agbar and Fòrum Building are examples of contemporary architecture that showcase the region's ongoing architectural evolution.

From Gaudí's organic creations to the intricate designs of Modernisme and the striking contrasts of contemporary architecture, Catalonia's art and architecture are a celebration of creativity and history.

Exploring Neighborhoods: El Born, Eixample, and Gràcia

Barcelona is a city full of diverse neighborhoods, each with its own unique flavor. El Born, Eixample, and Gràcia are three of the most popular districts, offering a mix of history, culture, and contemporary energy.

El Born

El Born is a lively and artistic area, renowned for its narrow medieval streets, stylish boutiques, and vibrant cafés. It's a cultural hub, home to attractions like the Picasso Museum and Museu de la Música. The Basilica de Santa Maria del Mar, a magnificent Gothic church, adds to the district's historical charm. Nearby, Parc de la Ciutadella offers a peaceful escape with greenery and open space. El Born effortlessly blends history, art, and modern vibrancy, making it a must-visit neighborhood.

Eixample

Eixample is known for its wide, grid-like streets, upscale shopping, and modernist architecture. This district is home to some of Gaudí's most iconic buildings, such as Casa Batlló and La Pedrera (Casa Milà), which line the elegant Passeig de Gràcia. Eixample offers a mixture of residential areas, commercial spaces, and a wealth of trendy cafés and restaurants. The spacious boulevards make it ideal for walking, and its central location provides easy access to the rest of the city.

Gràcia

Gràcia feels like a quaint village within Barcelona, with its cozy squares, independent stores, and relaxed atmosphere. Known for its cultural vibe, Gràcia hosts the lively Festa Major de Gràcia, a festival where the streets are beautifully decorated. The neighborhood is also home to Park Güell, one of Gaudí's most famous works, combining natural beauty with architectural brilliance. Gràcia's mix of local charm and artistic energy gives it a distinct, authentic feel, making it perfect for those looking to explore a more local side of Barcelona.

Each of these neighborhoods highlights a different aspect of Barcelona, El Born for its art and history, Eixample for its modernist beauty and shopping, and Gràcia for its relaxed, local atmosphere. Together, they offer a broad spectrum of what the city has to offer.

Beaches, Markets, and Nightlife

Catalonia offers a diverse range of experiences, from its beautiful beaches and vibrant markets to its dynamic nightlife. Whether you want to unwind by the sea, explore local culture, or enjoy the nightlife, Catalonia has something for everyone.

Beaches

The region's coastline boasts numerous stunning beaches, making it a prime destination for beach lovers. The Costa Brava is famous for its crystal-clear waters, rugged cliffs, and secluded coves, with towns like Cadaqués and Tossa de Mar offering both scenic beaches and charming atmospheres. Barcelona's beaches, such as Barceloneta, provide a more lively urban beach experience, complete with promenades, restaurants, and bars. Whether you're looking for relaxation or a lively beach vibe, Catalonia offers a variety of options.

Markets

The markets in Catalonia are a sensory delight, offering everything from fresh produce to local delicacies and unique souvenirs. La Boqueria Market in Barcelona is one of the most famous, where visitors can enjoy fresh seafood, artisan cheeses, and cured meats. Other markets like Mercat de Sant Antoni and Mercat de la Concepció also offer vibrant atmospheres and a wide selection of local products. Smaller markets in towns like Girona and Tarragona give visitors an authentic taste of Catalan cuisine and culture. Exploring these markets is a great way to experience the region's culinary traditions firsthand.

Nightlife

Catalonia's nightlife scene is diverse and exciting, especially in Barcelona, where the party scene is always alive. The city features an abundance of bars, clubs, and beachside spots, offering something for everyone. Neighborhoods like El Raval and El Born are known for their trendy bars, while Poble Sec offers a more relaxed atmosphere with tapas and live music venues. For those seeking to dance, Port Olímpic and Eixample offer clubs playing a mix of electronic music and Latin rhythms. If you prefer a quieter night out, you can enjoy a drink at a rooftop bar with scenic city views. Other cities like Girona and Tarragona also have a lively nightlife scene, with bars, music venues, and clubs catering to locals and tourists alike.

From the serene beaches of Costa Brava to the lively markets and bustling nightlife, Catalonia offers a wide range of experiences. Whether you're enjoying the beach, exploring local food, or dancing the night away, the region provides memorable experiences for all types of travelers.

CHAPTER 3: THE COSTA BRAVA

Best Beaches and Seaside Towns

The Costa Brava, located on the northeastern coast of Catalonia, is famous for its breathtaking beaches, clear waters, and charming coastal towns. Whether you're looking for a quiet escape, adventure, or a taste of local culture, these beaches and seaside towns offer something for every traveler.

Beaches

Cala Montjoi

A peaceful, secluded cove surrounded by pine trees, Cala Montjoi is ideal for those seeking a quiet day by the water. Its clear waters and serene atmosphere make it perfect for relaxation.

Platja de Pals

This spacious beach is a favorite for families and water sport enthusiasts. With its long stretch of golden sand and gentle waves, it's great for swimming, sunbathing, and enjoying the nearby beach bars and restaurants.

Cala Sa Boadella

Nestled near Lloret de Mar, Cala Sa Boadella is a quieter beach with crystal-clear waters and surrounded by cliffs and greenery. It's a peaceful retreat for those wanting to relax in a less crowded setting.

Platja de Castell

Located in Palamós, Platja de Castell is a beautiful, protected beach with golden sands and turquoise waters. Its peaceful surroundings, with scenic walking paths nearby, make it an ideal place for a quiet day at the beach.

Cala del Senyor Ramon

A small, hidden cove near Begur, Cala del Senyor Ramon is perfect for those seeking seclusion. Accessible by foot or boat, this beach is ideal for snorkeling and surrounded by dramatic cliffs and lush nature.

Seaside Towns

Cadaqués

Known for its whitewashed buildings, winding streets, and stunning sea views, Cadaqués is one of the most picturesque towns on the Costa Brava. Associated with Salvador Dalí, it offers a mix of art, history, and natural beauty, making it a perfect place for relaxing and exploring.

Tossa de Mar

With its medieval charm, Tossa de Mar is home to the historic Vila Vella (Old Town), which overlooks the beautiful Platja Gran beach. This town combines history, culture, and beautiful beaches, making it a popular choice for both history enthusiasts and beach lovers.

Begur

Surrounded by beautiful beaches and coves, Begur offers a blend of history, natural beauty, and Catalan charm. With stunning beaches like Cala Aiguablava and Cala d'Aiguafreda, it's an excellent destination for both relaxation and exploration, along with panoramic views of the coastline.

Palafrugell

Located near some of Costa Brava's best beaches, Palafrugell serves as an excellent base for exploring the region. Beautiful beaches like Cala de l'Illa Roja and Cala Estreta are nearby, and the town itself offers Mediterranean charm, with great restaurants serving fresh seafood.

L'Escala

With its ancient ruins at Empúries and it's lovely beaches like Platja de Riells and Cala Montgó, L'Escala is a town steeped in history and beauty. Its laid-back vibe and delicious local anchovies make it a great spot to enjoy Catalonia's coastal culture.

From tranquil beaches to picturesque towns, the Costa Brava is a must-visit for those wanting to experience the natural beauty and charm of Catalonia's coastline.

The Dalí Triangle: Figueres, Cadaqués, and Púbol

The Dalí Triangle is a captivating route in Catalonia that links three key locations associated with the life and art of Salvador Dalí: Figueres, Cadaqués, and Púbol. Each of these towns offers a unique perspective on Dalí's world, making them essential stops for anyone interested in his genius and legacy.

Figueres

Figueres, Dalí's birthplace, is home to the renowned Teatre-Museu Dalí, a must-see for art enthusiasts. The museum, designed by Dalí himself, is a surreal work of art in its own right, showcasing a vast collection of his paintings, sculptures, and personal belongings. From his early creations to his more experimental later works, the museum provides an immersive experience into Dalí's artistic evolution. The Teatre-Museu is more than just a museum, it's a tribute to Dalí's unconventional approach and creative vision.

Cadaqués

A short distance from Figueres, Cadaqués is a charming coastal town that Dalí often visited and found inspiring throughout his life. Its whitewashed buildings and narrow streets set against the Mediterranean Sea made it an ideal place for the artist. Dalí's connection to Cadaqués is strong, and his Casa Museu Dalí in the nearby Port Lligat was his residence for many years. The house is now a museum where visitors can explore Dalí's personal space, filled with his art, personal items, and quirky details that reflect his unique character and creative mind.

Púbol

The quiet village of Púbol, near La Bisbal d'Empordà, is where Dalí bought the Castell Gala Dalí for his wife Gala in the 1960s. The castle, now a museum, is dedicated to Gala and reveals Dalí's deep affection for her. The rooms are filled with Dalí's works and personal artifacts, providing a glimpse into his private life. Púbol is where Dalí spent much of his later years, and the peaceful, secluded setting of the castle offers a look into a more reflective time in his life.

Together, Figueres, Cadaqués, and Púbol create an extraordinary journey through the world of Salvador Dalí. The Dalí Triangle offers an intimate exploration of the places that shaped Dalí's creative journey and allows visitors to experience the lasting impact of his surreal art in Catalonia.

Outdoor Adventures: Snorkeling, Diving, and Coastal Walks

The Costa Brava is a haven for outdoor enthusiasts, offering an array of activities set against its stunning coastline. Whether you're drawn to underwater exploration or scenic hikes along the shore, the region provides ample opportunities to immerse yourself in nature.

Snorkeling

The Costa Brava's clear waters make it an ideal spot for snorkeling. Cala Montjoi near Roses is a top choice, with its calm, sheltered waters and diverse marine life. Cala Aigua Xelida, close to Tamariu, is another excellent location, where snorkelers can encounter a variety of sea creatures. For a truly unique experience, Cap de Creus Natural Park offers protected waters with a wealth of marine species, making it a must-visit for snorkeling enthusiasts.

Diving

For those interested in diving, the Costa Brava offers exceptional underwater experiences. The clear waters around Tossa de Mar and Palamós are teeming with marine life, including vibrant fish, sea turtles, and even shipwrecks. The Cap de Creus area is especially popular, with its underwater caves and dramatic rock formations. Many local diving centers in towns such as L'Escala and Roses provide guided dives and equipment rentals, making it easy to explore the underwater world.

Coastal Walks

The Costa Brava's rugged coastline is perfect for hiking, offering some of the most scenic trails in Catalonia. One of the highlights is the Camí de Ronda, a series of coastal paths that stretch from Blanes to Portbou. These trails offer spectacular views of the Mediterranean, passing by quiet beaches, hidden coves, and charming fishing villages. Another popular hike is around Cala Montjoi and Cala de la Canyella, where hikers can enjoy seclusion and picturesque vistas. For a more challenging hike, the Cap de Creus Natural Park provides rugged paths with sweeping views of the sea and dramatic landscapes.

From snorkeling in clear waters to diving among shipwrecks and hiking along the dramatic coastline, the Costa Brava offers endless outdoor adventures. With its unspoiled natural beauty, protected marine areas, and scenic trails, it's the perfect destination for those seeking both adventure and relaxation by the sea.

Hidden Villages and Scenic Drives

Beyond its stunning beaches, the Costa Brava is home to charming, lesser-known villages and some of the most scenic drives in Catalonia. These hidden gems allow you to experience the region's natural beauty and rich cultural heritage in a more peaceful, authentic setting.

Hidden Villages

Pals

Nestled on a hill, Pals is a beautifully preserved medieval village with cobblestone streets, historic stone buildings, and ancient watchtowers. Stroll through its quaint Old Town and enjoy breathtaking views of the surrounding countryside. Pals is also renowned for its local rice fields, which produce a unique variety featured in many regional dishes.

Peratallada

Located in the Baix Empordà region, Peratallada is another medieval treasure, surrounded by stone walls and narrow, winding lanes. The village is known for its historic charm, with lovely stone buildings and peaceful squares. It's a quiet and picturesque spot for a leisurely walk, offering a true taste of Catalan culture.

Begur

Though it's gaining popularity, Begur still feels like a hidden gem compared to other coastal towns. The village is famous for its Medieval Castle, which offers spectacular views of the surrounding landscape. With its whitewashed houses, cobbled streets, and lively squares, Begur is a perfect blend of history and coastal beauty, and nearby beaches like Cala Aiguablava offer a peaceful escape.

Castelló d'Empúries

Inland from the coast, Castelló d'Empúries is a small village rich in medieval history. The striking Gothic Church of Santa Maria is a standout, and the village's charming streets and squares make for an enjoyable exploration. It's also close to the Aiguamolls de l'Empordà Natural Park, a great spot for birdwatching and enjoying the area's natural beauty.

Scenic Drives

The C-66 from Girona to Palafrugell

This scenic route takes you through the heart of the Baix Empordà, passing through picturesque villages like Cassa de la Selva and Monells. The drive offers views of rolling hills, vineyards, and as you approach the coast, stunning vistas of the Mediterranean, providing a beautiful introduction to the Costa Brava.

The Coastal Road from Tossa de Mar to Lloret de Mar

One of the most scenic coastal routes, this drive from Tossa de Mar to Lloret de Mar winds along dramatic cliffs with sweeping sea views. The road takes you through forests and offers glimpses of hidden coves and beaches, making it a visually stunning route along the Costa Brava.

The GI-682: Begur to Aiguafreda

This winding road connects Begur to the picturesque beach of Aiguafreda and is a breathtaking drive along the coast. With views of the Mediterranean and rugged cliffs, the road is surrounded by lush Mediterranean flora, providing a peaceful and scenic experience.

The GI-550 from Palafrugell to Calella de Palafrugell

The GI-550 drive from Palafrugell to Calella de Palafrugell offers spectacular coastal views, with cliffs and hidden coves along the way. As you approach the village, the road offers panoramic vistas of the sparkling Mediterranean waters below, making this drive a memorable part of your Costa Brava journey.

The Costa Brava offers many scenic drives and charming villages waiting to be explored. From medieval towns with historic charm to stunning coastal routes, the region offers plenty of hidden treasures that are perfect for those wanting to discover its quieter, more authentic side.

CHAPTER 4: THE PYRENEES AND RURAL ESCAPES

Hiking, Skiing, and Adventure Sports

The Pyrenees, stretching along the border of Spain and France, are a top destination for outdoor lovers. From scenic hikes to thrilling skiing and extreme adventure sports, this mountain range offers something for every type of adventurer.

Hiking

The Pyrenees are filled with trails that suit all levels of hikers, from gentle strolls to more demanding mountain routes. The GR11, or Senda Pirenaica, runs along the southern edge of the range, offering hikers breathtaking views and diverse landscapes. For a less challenging but equally scenic experience, Ordesa and Monte Perdido National Park feature beautiful trails through lush forests and dramatic cliffs. For those looking for a true alpine adventure, the trail to Aneto, the highest peak in the range, provides an exciting challenge for seasoned hikers.

Skiing

The Pyrenees boast a variety of exceptional ski resorts, making them a great alternative to the Alps for winter sports. Baqueira-Beret in Spain's Val d'Aran is one of the region's top destinations, offering excellent slopes and modern amenities. The Formigal-Panticosa resort in the Aragonese Pyrenees caters to skiers of all levels with a vast network of runs, while Gourette in France is known for its varied terrain and welcoming atmosphere for families. Whether you're a beginner or an experienced skier, the Pyrenees provide a wide range of slopes, snowparks, and après-ski options.

Adventure Sports

For adrenaline junkies, the Pyrenees are an ideal location for a variety of thrilling activities. Canyoning is especially popular, with rivers that create dramatic gorges perfect for jumping, swimming, and climbing. Rafting and kayaking on rivers like the Garonne and Ariège offer exciting water adventures, while the rugged terrain is perfect for mountain biking. Paragliding provides an incredible way to see the mountains from above, offering stunning aerial views of the region's landscapes. Additionally, rock climbing and trail running are widely enjoyed, with many dedicated routes for those seeking more challenging pursuits.

From hiking across expansive trails to skiing on pristine slopes and engaging in thrilling sports, the Pyrenees offer endless opportunities for outdoor fun. With its rugged landscapes and diverse range of activities, the Pyrenees remain an unforgettable destination for adventure enthusiasts.

Picturesque Villages: Vall de Núria, Rupit, and Besalú

The regions around the Pyrenees are home to several idyllic villages, each offering a unique experience with their rich history and stunning landscapes. Among them, Vall de Núria, Rupit, and Besalú stand out for their beauty and distinct character.

Vall de Núria

Set high in the Pyrenees, Vall de Núria is a scenic village surrounded by dramatic mountains and lush meadows. Accessible only by a picturesque rack railway, the village is a peaceful haven. It's known for the sanctuary dedicated to the Virgin of Núria, drawing both spiritual visitors and nature enthusiasts. The breathtaking views of the mountains and nearby lake make it a perfect spot for hiking, skiing, or simply enjoying the tranquility of the area.

Rupit

Located in the Osona region, Rupit is a medieval village that exudes timeless charm. With its cobblestone streets, stone houses, and dramatic cliffs, Rupit offers a captivating atmosphere. The village is renowned for its medieval architecture, including the striking Rupit Bridge, which provides magnificent views of the surrounding landscape. Nature lovers can also explore the Cinglera de Rupit cliffs and nearby waterfalls, making it a great spot for both history and outdoor enthusiasts.

Besalú

In the Garrotxa region, Besalú is a medieval town that transports visitors back to another era. Known for its iconic Romanesque bridge, Besalú features narrow streets, ancient stone buildings, and charming plazas. The Jewish Quarter adds to the town's historical appeal, highlighting its rich cultural past. With its well-preserved medieval character and stunning surroundings, including the Olot Volcanic Zone, Besalú is a perfect place to immerse in history while enjoying the natural beauty around it.

Each of these villages offers a unique experience, whether you seek the peaceful mountain retreat of Vall de Núria, the medieval allure of Rupit, or the historic richness of Besalú. They are perfect examples of Catalonia's picturesque villages, each with its own distinct atmosphere and scenic charm.

National Parks and Wildlife Reserves

The Pyrenees are home to some of the most stunning national parks and wildlife reserves in both Spain and France. These protected areas showcase incredible landscapes and offer a rich variety of flora and fauna, making them ideal for nature lovers and adventure seekers.

Aigüestortes i Estany de Sant Maurici National Park

Located in the Spanish Pyrenees, Aigüestortes i Estany de Sant Maurici is renowned for its breathtaking beauty, featuring dramatic mountain peaks, lush valleys, and numerous glacial lakes, such as Sant Maurici Lake. The park is a hiker's paradise with trails offering magnificent views of its natural landscapes. Wildlife here includes brown bears, chamois, and various bird species.

Ordesa and Monte Perdido National Park

A UNESCO World Heritage site, Ordesa and Monte Perdido National Park spans both Spain and France. Known for its spectacular landscapes, the park includes steep gorges, alpine meadows, and towering mountains like Monte Perdido. It is home to rare species like the Pyrenean ibex and golden eagles and is a prime destination for hiking and wildlife spotting, with notable hikes to places like Circo de Soaso and Col de la Fache.

Pyrenees National Park (Parc National des Pyrénées)

Located on the French side of the Pyrenees, the Pyrenees National Park covers vast areas of diverse ecosystems, from lush valleys to rugged mountain peaks. It's a sanctuary for species such as the Pyrenean brown bear, vultures, and griffon eagles. The park is a hiker's dream, with trails leading to picturesque spots like Lac de Gaube, offering stunning vistas of the surrounding nature.

Cadi-Moixero Natural Park

Situated in the Spanish Catalan Pyrenees, Cadi-Moixero Natural Park is celebrated for its rugged landscapes and biodiversity. With steep cliffs, expansive forests, and deep valleys, it provides plenty of opportunities for outdoor exploration. The park is home to Pyrenean chamois, wild boars, and eagles, making it a great place for wildlife observation and hiking.

Vall de Sorteny National Park

Located in the Andorran Pyrenees, Vall de Sorteny Natural Park offers a peaceful natural retreat, featuring alpine meadows and rocky mountain peaks. The park is known for its rich flora, including wild orchids and edelweiss, and its diverse wildlife, such as marmots and red deer. It's a perfect spot for those seeking tranquility and natural beauty.

Mont Perdu and Cirque de Gavarnie

Part of the Ordesa and Monte Perdido National Park, the Cirque de Gavarnie is a dramatic natural wonder, with towering cliffs surrounding a waterfall that cascades into the valley below. Mont Perdu is another highlight of the region, known for its wildlife, including marmots, ibex, and various bird species. It's a great spot for hiking and wildlife watching, with several trails exploring the diverse terrain.

The national parks and wildlife reserves of the Pyrenees offer a wide array of landscapes, from lush valleys to rugged mountains, making them perfect for hiking, wildlife watching, and connecting with nature. Whether you're exploring Aigüestortes or spotting wildlife in Pyrenees National Park, the region provides endless opportunities for outdoor adventure.

Cultural Highlights in the Mountains

The Pyrenees Mountains are a treasure trove of cultural richness, blending natural beauty with a deep sense of history. Across the region, you'll find traditional villages, ancient monuments, and vibrant customs that reflect the diverse cultural influences of both Spain and France. Here are some of the key cultural highlights to explore.

Charming Villages and Historic Architecture

Many villages in the Pyrenees have preserved their historic charm, with cobblestone streets and traditional buildings. Aínsa, in the Spanish Aragon region, is a standout with its medieval castle, cobbled squares, and stone houses. Similarly, the French village of Saint-Lary-Soulan is known for its typical Pyrenean architecture, featuring wooden balconies and slate roofs, blending seamlessly with the mountain surroundings.

Romanesque Religious Sites

The region boasts a number of stunning Romanesque churches and monasteries that reveal its spiritual history. The San Juan de la Peña Monastery in Spain, carved into a cliffside, is an architectural marvel, while the Abbey of Saint-Just in Saint-Just, France, is famous for its beautiful frescoes and historical significance. These sacred sites provide an insight into the religious heritage of the Pyrenees.

Festivals and Traditions

The Pyrenees come alive with numerous festivals that celebrate local culture, music, and dance. One of the most well-known is the Fête de la Saint-Jean in Cauterets, France, which celebrates the start of summer with music, dance, and fire rituals. In Benasque, Spain, the Carnival celebrations feature vibrant costumes, parades, and lively street events. These festivals offer a fantastic opportunity to immerse yourself in the region's vibrant cultural traditions.

Local Cuisine

Cuisine plays a big role in the Pyrenees' cultural identity, with both Spain and France offering hearty, flavorful dishes perfect for the mountain climate. In Aragon, Spain, specialties like (roast lamb) and a la navarra (trout) are common, while the French side serves up dishes like garbure (a rich vegetable and pork soup) and tourte des Pyrénées (a savory pastry). The region's local ingredients and culinary traditions are integral to the Pyrenean experience.

Museums and Historical Landmarks

Several museums and historical landmarks throughout the Pyrenees offer a glimpse into the region's past. The Museo de los Pirineos en Jaca, Spain, provides exhibits on the history and natural environment of the mountains, while the Musée Pyrénéen in Lourdes, France, highlights local folk traditions, crafts, and art. Sites like the Château de Foix in France, a medieval castle once home to the

Counts of Foix, provide further insight into the region's rich history.

Pilgrimage Routes

The famous Camino de Santiago (Way of St. James), one of the world's most renowned pilgrimage routes, passes through the Pyrenees. Pilgrims can experience centuries of religious and cultural tradition as they follow the route, encountering ancient chapels, historic towns, and breathtaking mountain landscapes along the way.

Linguistic and Cultural Diversity

The Pyrenees are a melting pot of languages and cultural influences. In the Spanish Pyrenees, Catalan is spoken in the northeastern regions, while Occitan, a dialect of French, is still spoken in some rural areas of France. These languages are closely tied to local customs, with traditions passed down through generations, enriching the cultural fabric of the Pyrenees.

The Pyrenees offer more than just spectacular natural scenery; they also provide a rich cultural journey. From historic villages and churches to lively festivals and traditional cuisine, the cultural highlights of this region are an essential part of the Pyrenean experience.

CHAPTER 5: HISTORIC CITIES – GIRONA AND TARRAGONA

Girona: Medieval Streets and Modern Charm

Located in northeastern Catalonia, Girona offers a unique fusion of historical charm and contemporary vitality. With its medieval streets, historic landmarks, and dynamic cultural scene, this city is a captivating destination.

The Historic Old Town (Barri Vell)

The heart of Girona lies in its Old Town (Barri Vell), where winding cobblestone streets, centuries-old buildings, and picturesque squares create a captivating atmosphere. The Girona Cathedral, with its stunning Gothic architecture, stands as a major highlight. Exploring the Jewish Quarter (El Call), one of Europe's best-preserved, offers a glimpse into the city's rich past. The Arab Baths, influenced by Roman styles, provide a fascinating insight into Girona's diverse history.

Medieval Walls and Scenic Views

Girona's impressive Medieval Walls are among the best-preserved in Spain. Walking along the Passeig de la Muralla pathway offers incredible views over the city and beyond, with striking perspectives of the Old Town and its historic structures.

The Onyar River and Colorful Architecture

The Onyar River flows through Girona, with its distinctive colorful houses lining the banks. One of the best views of these vibrant buildings is from the Pont de Ferro (Iron Bridge). This area, with its lively cafes and shops, provides a perfect spot to relax and enjoy the scenic surroundings.

Modern Girona

While Girona is rich in history, it also embraces modernity. The tranquil La Devesa Park offers expansive green spaces perfect for a peaceful escape. Additionally, Girona has a thriving contemporary art scene, with museums like the Museu d'Art de Girona, showcasing both medieval and modern artistic works.

Gastronomy and Local Flavors

Food lovers will find plenty to enjoy in Girona. The city's culinary scene blends traditional Catalan dishes with creative modern influences. Renowned restaurants like El Celler de Can Roca are world-famous, while local eateries offer favorites such as (stuffed pasta) and (fried dough treats). The Girona food market is also a must-visit for fresh produce and local specialties.

Festivals and Celebrations

Girona is home to many vibrant festivals that celebrate the city's culture and traditions. Temps de Flors, the Flower Festival, fills the city with breathtaking floral displays. Another major event is the Festa Major de Girona, a summer celebration featuring parades, music, and dancing, bringing the city's festive energy to life.

Girona beautifully merges its medieval heritage with a modern vibrancy. Its historic streets, thriving arts scene, and gastronomic delights make it a must-see city in Catalonia, offering something for every type of traveler. Whether wandering through ancient walls or exploring contemporary art, Girona promises a memorable experience.

The Cathedral, Jewish Quarter, and River Onyar

Girona is a city that beautifully blends history, culture, and scenic beauty, and its Cathedral, Jewish Quarter, and Onyar River are three of its most iconic landmarks.

Girona Cathedral

Standing tall over the city, the Girona Cathedral is a stunning example of Gothic architecture, famous for its grand staircase that leads up to its entrance. Inside, the cathedral features the world's widest Gothic nave, creating a breathtaking space. It also houses the Tapestry of Creation, an important medieval artifact. The cathedral's design incorporates Romanesque, Gothic, and Baroque elements, making it a unique architectural gem.

The Jewish Quarter (El Call)

One of the best-preserved in Europe, the Jewish Quarter (El Call) offers a glimpse into Girona's medieval Jewish history. Its narrow, winding streets and well-maintained buildings reflect the once-thriving Jewish community in the city. The Museum of Jewish History further explores this rich heritage. Strolling through the quarter, visitors can experience its ancient alleys and sense the history that lingers in the air.

The Onyar River and Its Vibrant Houses

The Onyar River, which flows through Girona, is flanked by the city's famous colorful houses, creating one of the most picturesque scenes in the city. The Pont de Ferro (Iron Bridge) provides an excellent spot to take in the view of the river and its bright, pastel-hued buildings. This area is also home to charming cafes and walking paths, perfect for a leisurely stroll and enjoying the river's beauty.

Together, the Cathedral, the Jewish Quarter, and the Onyar River embody the charm and historical depth of Girona, where history, culture, and stunning landscapes come together to create an unforgettable experience.

Tarragona: Roman Heritage on the Coast

Situated along Catalonia's Mediterranean coast, Tarragona is a city rich in history, where its Roman past shines through in well-preserved ruins and stunning seaside views. A perfect destination for history enthusiasts and those seeking both cultural and natural beauty, Tarragona offers an unforgettable experience.

Roman Monuments and Ancient Sites

Tarragona is home to some of Spain's most significant Roman remains. Once the capital of Roman Hispania Citerior, the city's archaeological landmarks are a window into its glorious past. The Roman Amphitheatre, right by the coast, is one of the most impressive sites, where gladiator games once took place. Other notable ruins include the Roman Circus, Forum, and the Roman Walls, offering a deep dive into the daily life of the Romans.

Tarragona's Archaeological Museum

To further explore the city's Roman legacy, the Archaeological Museum of Tarragona is essential. It houses a rich collection of artifacts, such as sculptures, pottery, and inscriptions, many of which were unearthed during the city's archaeological excavations. The museum provides an in-depth look at the Roman era and its profound impact on the region.

Stunning Mediterranean Beaches

Tarragona is not only about history but also boasts beautiful beaches along the Mediterranean coastline. Platja del Miracle and other nearby beaches offer the perfect spot to unwind after exploring the ancient ruins. With clear waters and scenic views of the Roman structures by the sea, these beaches provide a tranquil escape.

Charming Old Town and Modern Vibes

The city's Old Town is a delightful maze of narrow streets, bustling squares, and local life. Carrer

Major, a pedestrian street, is filled with quaint shops, cafes, and restaurants serving delicious Catalan cuisine. Tarragona also has a modern side, with lively arts, shopping areas, and cafes that offer a laid-back atmosphere.

Festivals and Cultural Events

Tarragona's lively festivals celebrate its Roman and cultural heritage. The Tarraco Viva Festival brings the ancient Roman world to life with reenactments, performances, and exhibits. The Festa Major, a summer celebration, fills the streets with parades, music, and fireworks, creating a festive and vibrant atmosphere in the city.

Tarragona seamlessly blends its rich Roman history with the relaxed charm of the Mediterranean. From ancient ruins to beautiful beaches and a thriving local culture, it's a city where history and modern life come together in perfect harmony.

Amphitheater, Forum, and UNESCO Sites

Tarragona is a treasure trove of Roman heritage, and its remarkable Amphitheater, Forum, and UNESCO-listed sites offer a fascinating glimpse into the city's ancient past.

Roman Amphitheater

The Roman Amphitheater in Tarragona is one of the most impressive and iconic landmarks of the city. Located right by the Mediterranean coast, it once hosted gladiatorial combat and other public spectacles for thousands of spectators. The structure, built in the 2nd century AD, is remarkably well-preserved, and visitors can explore the arena where ancient Romans gathered to watch dramatic events. The view of the amphitheater against the backdrop of the sea makes it one of Tarragona's most photogenic sites.

The Roman Forum

The Roman Forum in Tarragona, once the center of civic life, is another key site that transports visitors back to Roman times. Located in the heart of the city, the forum was the place where political, social, and religious activities took place. Though much of it is now in ruins, the site still conveys the grandeur of what was once one of the most important areas of the Roman Empire. Visitors can explore the remains of temples, basilicas, and public buildings, offering a window into the daily life of ancient Romans.

UNESCO World Heritage Sites

Tarragona's Roman ruins are so significant that they have been designated as a UNESCO World Heritage Site. In 2000, the Archaeological Ensemble of Tarraco was recognized for its exceptional preservation and historical importance. The UNESCO designation covers a wide range of archaeological sites across the city, including the Amphitheater, Roman Circus, Forum, Roman Walls, and the Aqueduct. These sites represent one of the most complete and best-preserved collections of Roman architecture and urban planning in the Mediterranean.

Together, the Amphitheater, Forum, and UNESCO World Heritage Sites of Tarragona showcase the city's rich Roman past. These landmarks, preserved through the centuries, provide visitors with a unique opportunity to experience ancient history in a modern setting.

Local Cuisine and Historical Tours

Tarragona seamlessly blends its rich history with a vibrant culinary scene, providing visitors with the opportunity to explore ancient landmarks while savoring traditional Catalan dishes.

Savoring Local Flavors

Tarragona's local cuisine draws heavily from Mediterranean influences, with a focus on fresh seafood and regional specialties. Popular dishes include romesco sauce, often paired with grilled fish or meats, and calçots, a variety of green onions typically grilled and served with romesco. The city's restaurants and taverns offer a cozy atmosphere where you can enjoy these authentic flavors. Additionally, Tarragona is renowned for its fine wines, especially those from the nearby Priorat and Tarragona wine regions, making them ideal companions for a meal.

Exploring Tarragona's History

Tarragona's rich historical heritage is best discovered through its Roman ruins and guided tours. Highlights include visits to the Roman Amphitheater, Roman Circus, and the Forum, where expert guides offer fascinating insights into the city's ancient past. The Archaeological Museum further enhances the experience with its extensive collection of artifacts, offering visitors a deeper understanding of Tarragona's role as the capital of Roman Hispania Citerior.

Tarragona's combination of local cuisine and historical tours creates a unique experience, appealing to both food lovers and history enthusiasts.

CHAPTER 6: CATALAN CUISINE AND GASTRONOMY

Traditional Dishes: Pa amb Tomàquet, Escudella, and Crema Catalana

Pa amb Tomàquet

This quintessential dish is a cornerstone of Catalan cuisine. It's made by rubbing ripe tomatoes on toasted or grilled rustic bread, then drizzling it with high-quality olive oil and sprinkling it with salt. Often paired with toppings like jamón ibérico, anchovies, or manchego cheese, it began as a way to make stale bread more appetizing and has since become a beloved tradition.

Escudella i Carn d'Olla

One of Europe's oldest stews, Escudella is a hearty meal often enjoyed in winter or on special occasions like Christmas. It's traditionally served in two parts: the flavorful broth, which includes noodles or rice, and the solid components, such as pork, beef, chicken, vegetables, and the "," a large spiced meatball. This dish embodies the region's emphasis on shared meals and festive traditions.

Crema Catalana

Often regarded as Europe's oldest dessert, Crema Catalana is a creamy custard made with milk, egg yolks, sugar, and cornstarch, flavored with lemon zest and cinnamon. It's topped with a layer of caramelized sugar, creating a delightful contrast between the smooth custard and the crunchy topping. Traditionally, the caramelization is done with a hot iron, adding an authentic touch. This dessert is especially popular on Saint Joseph's Day (March 19).

Wine Regions: Penedès, Priorat, and Empordà

Penedès

Located southwest of Barcelona, Penedès is a diverse wine region renowned for its production of Cava, Spain's sparkling wine made using the traditional method. The primary grapes, Macabeo, Xarel·lo, and Parellada are essential for Cava, but the region also produces excellent still wines, including whites like Chardonnay and reds like Tempranillo.

Climate and Terrain: Penedès features three subzones, coastal, middle, and high altitudes, allowing for a wide range of grape varieties. The higher areas are known for crisp whites, while lower zones focus on reds and sparkling wines.

Experience: Visitors can explore vineyards, enjoy Cava tastings, and learn about sustainable winemaking. Sant Sadurní d'Anoia, the heart of Cava production, is a highlight.

Priorat

This small yet prestigious region in Tarragona is famous for its powerful, full-bodied red wines. Its distinctive soil, volcanic slate, gives the wines a unique minerality.

Grapes: The main varieties are Garnacha (Grenache) and Cariñena (Carignan), often blended with international grapes like Syrah and Cabernet

Sauvignon. These wines are bold, intense, and age beautifully.

Reputation: As one of only two regions in Spain with the top-tier DOCa classification, Priorat is highly respected globally.

Experience: Visitors can admire the terraced vineyards, tour historic cellars, and taste wines while learning about the region's labor-intensive winemaking process.

Empordà

Located in Catalonia's northeastern corner along the Costa Brava, Empordà has a winemaking tradition that dates back over 2,500 years to Greek settlers.

Wines: The region offers a variety of reds, whites, rosés, and sweet dessert wines. Garnacha (Grenache) and Cariñena are key red varieties, while whites often feature Macabeo and Muscat, creating fresh, aromatic wines.

Climate and Soil: Mediterranean breezes and the Tramuntana winds help maintain grape health and freshness, while sandy and granitic soils add a mineral quality to the wines.

Experience: Empordà's picturesque coastal vineyards and charming villages make it a delightful destination. Visitors can enjoy tastings at family-run wineries and pair the wines with local dishes like seafood and cured meats.

Cava Tasting: The Sparkling Wine of Catalonia

Cava, Catalonia's iconic sparkling wine, is a must-try for wine lovers. Made using the traditional Champagne method, it features local grape varieties like Macabeo, Xarel·lo, and Parellada, giving it a unique flavor profile.

Why Cava Stands Out

Variety of Styles: From the crisp and dry Brut Nature to the rich and layered Gran Reserva, there's a Cava to suit any taste.

Affordable Excellence: Cava offers the craftsmanship of Champagne without the hefty price tag.

Regional Character: Produced in the Penedès region, its Mediterranean climate, diverse soils, and altitudes contribute to the wine's complexity and depth.

Best Places for Cava Tasting

The town of Sant Sadurní d'Anoia, located about an hour from Barcelona, is the heart of Cava production. Here, you can visit well-known wineries like Codorníu and Freixenet to tour their cellars and enjoy tastings. Smaller, family-run vineyards in the Penedès region also offer more personal experiences, often paired with local delicacies like cheese and charcuterie.

Perfect Pairings

Cava's versatility makes it an excellent companion to various dishes, from tapas and seafood to desserts. Its effervescence and bright flavors enhance almost any meal.

Markets, Tapas Bars, and Michelin-Starred Restaurants

Markets

The region's markets are a sensory delight. In Barcelona, La Boqueria is a bustling market where you can find everything from fresh produce to seafood and gourmet treats. For a more authentic experience, Mercat de Sant Antoni and Mercat de la Concepció offer a local vibe with regional specialties. These markets are perfect for sampling everything from jamón ibérico to churros.

Tapas Bars

Tapas bars in Catalonia are perfect for enjoying a variety of small dishes. El Xampanyet is a great spot to try traditional tapas paired with Cava, while Bar Cañete serves creative takes on classic tapas. These casual bars are ideal for sampling everything from patatas bravas to more inventive small plates.

Michelin-Starred Restaurants

For a fine dining experience, Catalonia is home to several Michelin-starred restaurants. El Celler de

Can Roca in Girona, known for its innovative cuisine, offers an exceptional dining experience. In Barcelona, Lasarte and Moments stand out for their cutting-edge dishes, blending traditional Catalan flavors with modern techniques for an unforgettable meal.

CHAPTER 7: FESTIVALS AND CULTURAL TRADITIONS

Iconic Events: La Mercè, Castells, and Sant Jordi

La Mercè

When and Where: La Mercè takes place every September in Barcelona, primarily around Plaza de España and Parc de la Ciutadella.

What to Expect: This lively festival features outdoor concerts, performances, art exhibits, and traditional Catalan rituals like castells (human towers), sardanas (dancing), and the exciting correfoc (fire runs). A standout event is the Piromusical, a spectacular fireworks show synchronized with music at Montjuïc.

Tips: Arrive early to find good spots for the fireworks or live performances. Don't miss out on visiting the parks where various events take place, such as Parc de la Ciutadella.

Castells

When and Where: Castells are performed throughout the year, with notable events in Valls (the birthplace of castells), Tarragona, and Barcelona. The Concurs de Castells in Tarragona, held biennially, is one of the key events.

What to Expect: Watch as human teams build towering, multi-tiered human structures that can reach impressive heights. The atmosphere is charged with anticipation as the teams carefully build and balance these intricate formations.

Tips: If attending the Concurs de Castells, arrive early for the best viewing spots. Take some time to learn about the structure and roles within a castle to enhance your understanding and appreciation.

Sant Jordi

When and Where: Celebrated on April 23 across Catalonia, Las Ramblas and Passeig de Gracia in Barcelona are prime locations for the festivities.

What to Expect: The streets are lined with stalls selling roses and books, and people exchange gifts of roses and literature, making it a celebration of both love and culture. Local authors often attend book signings, and there are many literary events throughout the day.

Tips: If you're interested in Catalan literature, seek out books by local authors or visit libraries hosting special events. It's a perfect day to explore the cultural side of Barcelona, including literary cafés and museums.

Folklore, Music, and Dance

Catalonia's cultural landscape is enriched by its vibrant folklore, music, and dance traditions, which are central to the region's identity and often featured during local festivals and public celebrations.

Folklore

Catalan folklore is full of legendary figures and tales passed down through generations. Famous characters include the Caganer, a traditional figurine often included in nativity scenes, and La Dama de Elche, an ancient Iberian goddess. Local legends, such as the tale of Sant Jordi (Saint

George) slaying the dragon, also play a significant role in Catalan cultural celebrations and festivals.

Music

Catalonia's music spans a wide range of genres, from traditional folk to modern styles. The sardana, a traditional dance accompanied by live music, is particularly noteworthy. It's performed with instruments like the (a wind instrument) and cymbals, played by an ensemble, creating an inviting atmosphere for community participation. Another important music genre is nova cançó (new song), which emerged in the 1960s, combining folk influences with political themes, and continues to impact the music scene today.

Dance

The sardana is the quintessential Catalan dance, where dancers form a circle and hold hands. It represents both social unity and cultural pride. During festivals like La Mercè and Festa Major, participants of all ages gather in public squares to dance the sardana. In addition, the giants and big heads (gegants i), oversized puppets featured in parades, are a playful and theatrical component of Catalan celebrations.

Festivals and Celebrations

La Mercè: In addition to castles (human towers) and parades, La Mercè is a great time for enjoying sardana dancing and traditional music performances.

Festa Major: These town celebrations across Catalonia are marked by folk music, dance, and other folkloric traditions, including gegants and castellers.

Folk Music Festivals: Events like the Festival Internacional de Música de Santes Creus and the Festival de la Sardana showcase traditional music, often held in scenic, historic locations.

Immersing in Catalan Folklore

To fully experience Catalan folklore, attending local festivals is key. These events let you join in the sardana dance, witness castles, and enjoy folk music, providing a deeper understanding of Catalan culture and community life.

Local Celebrations and Seasonal Festivals

Catalonia is known for its lively local celebrations and seasonal festivals, each offering a unique glimpse into the region's rich traditions and vibrant community life. These events allow visitors to experience Catalan culture throughout the year.

Winter and Spring Festivals

Carnaval (February/March): Catalonia celebrates Carnaval with vibrant parades, costumes, and street parties. Notable festivals include Sitges, renowned for its festive atmosphere and LGBTQ+ inclusivity, and Vilanova i la Geltrú, known for its elaborate floats and lively street dances.

Festa de la Candelera (February 2): Celebrated in Cervera, this festival marks the transition from winter to spring with bonfires, processions, and festivities that signal the end of the cold season.

Sant Jordi (April 23): Catalonia's version of Valentine's Day, Sant Jordi celebrates love and literature with streets filled with stalls selling roses and books. Couples exchange gifts, and authors participate in book signings, creating a festive atmosphere.

Summer Festivals

Festa Major (Late June to August): This is a season of celebrations across Catalonia, with each town hosting its own Festa Major in honor of its patron saint. These festivals feature music, dancing, fireworks, parades, and castells (human towers). The Festa Major de Gràcia in Barcelona is particularly famous for its street decorations and neighborhood parties.

Nit de Sant Joan (June 23-24): Marking the summer solstice, this celebration is filled with bonfires, fireworks, and beach parties along the Catalan coast. Cities like Barcelona and Sitges host all-night festivities to welcome the summer season.

Autumn Festivals

La Mercè (September): Barcelona's largest festival celebrates the city's patron saint, featuring parades, fireworks, and traditional Catalan performances such as castells and correfoc (fire runs). It is one of the most well-known and eagerly anticipated festivals in the region.

Festa de la Verema (September): Held in the Penedès and Priorat wine regions, this festival celebrates the grape harvest with wine tastings, local food, and folk music, offering visitors a taste of Catalonia's rich wine culture.

Year-Round Celebrations

Castells Competitions (Various Dates): Major competitions, like the Concurs de Castells in Tarragona every two years, showcase the strength and precision of human tower teams from across Catalonia.

Diada de Catalunya (September 11): Catalonia's National Day commemorates the fall of Barcelona in 1714 during the War of Spanish Succession. The day is marked by large demonstrations, political rallies, and cultural activities celebrating Catalan identity.

Experiencing Catalan Festivals

Attending Catalonia's festivals is an ideal way to immerse yourself in the region's culture. These events reflect the community's history, traditions, and shared spirit. Whether you're watching a castell, joining a sardana dance, or enjoying a street parade, there's something for everyone to experience year-round.

Experiencing Catalonia's Vibrant Community Spirit

The community spirit in Catalonia is an integral part of its culture, deeply reflected in local events, festivals, and daily life. To truly understand Catalonia, engaging with its communal activities offers a unique way to connect with the region's essence.

Festivals and Celebrations

Catalan festivals are the perfect expression of the region's lively and inclusive atmosphere. Events like La Mercè, Sant Jordi, and Festa Major bring people together, promoting a sense of shared celebration and pride. Whether it's participating in a sardana dance, cheering for a castell (human tower), or experiencing the fiery excitement of a correfoc, these events invite everyone to be part of a larger community experience that celebrates collective identity.

Human Towers (Castells)

Castells, or human towers, showcase Catalonia's communal values of cooperation and trust. Teams, called colles, build towering structures of people, demonstrating teamwork, balance, and strength. These performances highlight the collective effort that defines Catalan culture, working together to achieve something extraordinary. Witnessing a castell during a local festival is a powerful reminder of the unity that binds the community.

Sardana Dancing

The sardana dance is another symbol of Catalonia's community spirit. Performed in a circle, with participants holding hands, it reflects the region's emphasis on unity and togetherness. The dance, accompanied by live music from a cobla ensemble, invites everyone—locals and visitors alike, to join in, turning public spaces into lively, communal celebrations.

Community Markets and Social Spaces

Local markets, like La Boqueria in Barcelona, serve as more than just places to buy food, they are lively hubs where people gather, talk, and connect. These markets reflect the Catalan tradition of socializing and fostering a sense of belonging, offering a glimpse into daily life and the region's strong community ties.

Local Traditions and Values

Catalonia's culture is built on values such as solidarity, cooperation, and mutual respect. These principles are not only seen in festivals but also in everyday interactions. Whether it's working together to build a castell or enjoying a local tradition, these values foster a deep sense of community.

The Catalan Way of Life

Experiencing Catalonia's community spirit extends beyond festivals—it's found in simple daily moments. Whether enjoying a meal with friends, participating in a local custom, or chatting with neighbors, the communal energy is always present. The pride in local culture and history is evident in how Catalans connect with one another and with visitors.

Immersing Yourself in Catalonia's Spirit

To truly connect with Catalonia's community spirit, take part in a local festival, join a sardana dance, or attend a castell performance. Visiting local markets or neighborhood events will also give you an authentic feel for the region's way of life. Engaging with the community and its traditions will provide a deeper understanding of Catalonia's cultural fabric.

CHAPTER 8: OUTDOOR ADVENTURES AND NATURAL WONDERS

Montserrat: The Iconic Mountain and Monastery

Montserrat, one of Catalonia's most famous landmarks, is a stunning mountain range located just outside Barcelona. Known for its dramatic rock formations and religious significance, it offers a perfect blend of natural beauty and historical importance, making it a must-see destination.

The Mountain

The name "Montserrat" means "serrated mountain" in Catalan, which describes its distinctive, jagged peaks. Standing at 1,236 meters (4,055 feet), the mountain provides breathtaking views of the surrounding valleys and plains. Its unique rock formations, shaped by erosion over millennia, are a draw for both nature lovers and geologists.

The Monastery of Montserrat

At the peak of the mountain sits the Monastery of Montserrat, a spiritual center founded in the 11th century. The monastery is dedicated to the Virgin of Montserrat, whose statue, La Moreneta (The Black Madonna), resides in the Basilica of Montserrat. The image is a significant symbol of Catalan devotion and is believed to have miraculous powers. Visitors come to admire the statue and experience the tranquility of the site.

History and Culture

The Monastery of Montserrat has played a key role in Catalan history as a hub for education, art, and religion. Benedictine monks still live at the monastery today, continuing the practice of daily prayer and devotion. The monastery also features a museum with works by famous artists like El Greco, Picasso, and Dalí, enriching the experience with a cultural dimension.

Hiking and Nature

Montserrat is a paradise for nature lovers, with a variety of hiking trails that offer stunning views of the surrounding landscape. There are routes for all levels of hikers, including the popular Santa Cova trail, which leads to a cave where the Virgin of Montserrat was said to be discovered. For those looking for an easier way to access the higher points, a funicular or cable car provides a scenic and effortless ride.

Visiting Montserrat

Montserrat is easily reachable from Barcelona, making it a popular destination for a day trip. Whether you come for its religious significance, its breathtaking views, or its cultural treasures, Montserrat promises a rewarding experience. The combination of awe-inspiring landscapes, historical depth, and spiritual calm make it one of Catalonia's most beloved landmarks.

National and Natural Parks: Aiguamolls de l'Empordà, Montseny, and Garrotxa

Catalonia boasts a wealth of natural parks, each offering distinct landscapes and ecosystems. Among the most renowned are Aiguamolls de l'Empordà, Montseny, and Garrotxa, which highlight the region's ecological diversity and natural charm.

Aiguamolls de l'Empordà Natural Park

Located in the northeastern part of Catalonia, near the Mediterranean coastline, Aiguamolls de l'Empordà is a protected wetland area known for its rich birdlife. Covering over 4,700 hectares of marshes, lagoons, and reed beds, it is one of Catalonia's key bird reserves. The park is especially popular with birdwatchers during migration seasons, offering sightings of species like herons, flamingos, and ospreys. With its peaceful ambiance, scenic trails, and observation points, Aiguamolls de l'Empordà provides a perfect nature retreat.

Montseny Natural Park

As a UNESCO Biosphere Reserve, Montseny is one of Catalonia's most celebrated natural parks. Situated just north of Barcelona, it features a diverse landscape of mountains, forests, and varied ecosystems. From Mediterranean scrubland to temperate woodlands, Montseny is home to numerous plant and animal species, including the rare Montseny salamander and Spanish wild goat. The park is ideal for hiking, with numerous trails that offer stunning views and opportunities to explore picturesque villages and pristine nature.

Garrotxa Volcanic Zone Natural Park

Located in Girona, Garrotxa Volcanic Zone is a dramatic landscape of over 40 volcanic cones and more than 20 lava flows. This park is renowned for its lush green valleys, volcanic craters, and diverse wildlife. Its dense beech forests, including the famous Fageda d'en Jordà, which grows on volcanic terrain, create a magical atmosphere. In addition to its geological wonders, Garrotxa offers cultural treasures, with charming medieval towns and historical churches dotting the landscape.

Discovering Catalonia's Natural Parks

These parks provide the perfect setting for outdoor activities, offering a unique opportunity to connect with Catalonia's natural environment. Whether you're birdwatching in Aiguamolls de l'Empordà, hiking the trails of Montseny, or exploring the volcanic landscapes of Garrotxa, each park offers an unforgettable experience of Catalonia's rich biodiversity and natural beauty.

Scenic Routes: Coastal Walks and Biking Trails

Catalonia is a paradise for outdoor enthusiasts, offering a variety of scenic routes for walking and biking that highlight the region's natural beauty. From stunning coastal paths to scenic biking trails, these routes provide the perfect opportunity to explore Catalonia's diverse landscapes, including rugged cliffs, pristine beaches, and charming coastal towns.

Coastal Walks

Catalonia's Mediterranean coastline is famous for its breathtaking scenery. One of the most popular walking trails is the Cami de Ronda, a series of coastal paths offering sweeping views of the sea, dramatic cliffs, and hidden coves. This route connects several coastal towns, including Cadaqués,

Tossa de Mar, and Calella de Palafrugell, making it a great option for exploring charming villages along the way. Whether you're looking for a short walk or a longer trek, the Cami de Ronda offers a stunning way to experience the Catalan coast.

For a more tranquil experience, the Cap de Creus Natural Park provides peaceful coastal walks with spectacular views of the Mediterranean. Its rugged terrain, dotted with quiet beaches and crystal-clear waters, makes it an ideal place for a serene escape.

Biking Trails

Catalonia is also home to a wide range of biking trails, from easy coastal routes to more challenging mountain paths. The Greenways of Catalonia (Vias Verdes) is a network of former railway lines converted into scenic biking trails. These trails wind through beautiful towns, forests, and vineyards, offering an ideal route for leisurely cycling trips.

For those seeking more adventure, the Pyrenees offer challenging mountain biking trails with dramatic views. The Cava Route in the Penedès wine region is another excellent biking option, combining scenic vineyard landscapes with visits to local wineries where you can taste Catalonia's famous Cava wine.

Discovering Catalonia by Bike or Foot

Whether you prefer a leisurely stroll along the coast or an exciting mountain biking adventure, Catalonia has countless scenic routes to explore its natural wonders. From coastal paths like the Cami de Ronda to peaceful hikes in Cap de Creus, and cycling trails through the Vias Verdes or the Pyrenees, there are plenty of options for immersing yourself in the Catalan landscape.

Eco-Tourism and Wildlife

Catalonia is a prime destination for eco-tourism, offering travelers the chance to experience its diverse landscapes and rich biodiversity while supporting sustainable practices. From coastal areas to mountains and wetlands, the region's natural beauty is ideal for those looking to explore nature responsibly.

Natural Reserves and Protected Areas

The region is home to several protected areas and reserves that focus on conserving its unique ecosystems. Notable parks such as Aiguamolls de l'Empordà and Montseny provide both scenic beauty and essential habitats for wildlife. Aiguamolls de l'Empordà, for example, serves as a crucial stop for migratory birds and offers guided tours for bird enthusiasts. Montseny, recognized as a UNESCO Biosphere Reserve, features a variety of ecosystems, including Mediterranean forests and alpine meadows, making it perfect for those seeking to connect with nature.

Wildlife Watching

Catalonia's varied habitats offer abundant opportunities for wildlife observation. In the Pyrenees, you can spot animals such as the Spanish wild goat, brown bears, and golden eagles. The Ebro Delta is a hotspot for birdwatching, with species like flamingos, herons, and ospreys populating its wetlands. Travelers can enjoy eco-friendly activities like nature walks, boat tours, and guided excursions to observe wildlife in its natural habitat.

Sustainable Travel and Green Practices

Eco-tourism in Catalonia goes beyond natural parks and wildlife. The region promotes sustainable travel through initiatives like eco-friendly accommodations, green transportation, and responsible tourism. Many hotels and accommodations have adopted practices such as using renewable energy, recycling, and offering locally-sourced organic food. Cycling and walking tours are also encouraged, allowing visitors to explore the region's beauty while minimizing their environmental impact.

Eco-Friendly Activities

Catalonia offers numerous eco-friendly activities that allow you to enjoy its natural wonders while protecting the environment. Cycling along the Vias Verdes (Greenways), a network of former railways transformed into scenic bike trails, is a great way to experience the region's countryside sustainably. Kayaking, hiking, and wildlife photography also provide opportunities to appreciate Catalonia's landscapes without disturbing its ecosystems.

Conserving Catalonia's Natural Treasures

Eco-tourism in Catalonia is centered on sustainability and conservation. Local efforts focus on preserving natural habitats, protecting wildlife, and promoting responsible travel. By engaging in eco-friendly activities, supporting local conservation initiatives, and respecting nature, visitors can contribute to safeguarding the region's landscapes and wildlife.

Planning Your Eco-Friendly Visit

To fully enjoy your ecotourism experience in Catalonia, consider visiting its natural parks, wildlife reserves, and protected areas. Choose guided tours that emphasize environmental education and conservation, and explore the region by bike, foot, or boat to minimize your impact. Whether you're birdwatching in Aiguamolls de l'Empordà, hiking in Montseny, or cycling through rural landscapes, Catalonia offers countless ways to connect with nature sustainably.

CHAPTER 9: FAMILY-FRIENDLY CATALONIA

Theme Parks: PortAventura and Tibidabo

PortAventura: Mediterranean Excitement

Located near Salou, PortAventura World is a hotspot for thrill-seekers and families. The park features six themed zones like Mediterrània, Far West, and Polynesia. Top attractions include Shambhala, Europe's tallest roller coaster, and the loop-filled Dragon Khan. For water fun, Caribe Aquatic Park offers slides and lazy rivers, while Ferrari Land showcases speed and luxury in true Ferrari style.

Tibidabo: Barcelona's Timeless Treasure

Set atop a hill with stunning views of Barcelona, Tibidabo Amusement Park is a charming, historic escape. Open since 1901, it's one of the world's oldest theme parks. Enjoy the vintage carousel, the iconic Avió ride, or the colorful Ferris wheel, all with breathtaking city vistas. The nearby Temple Expiatori del Sagrat Cor adds a spiritual and architectural highlight to your trip.

PortAventura delivers high-energy thrills, while Tibidabo offers a nostalgic, scenic experience, two very different but equally memorable destinations.

Kid-Friendly Beaches and Outdoor Activities

Family-Friendly Beaches in Catalonia
Barceloneta Beach (Barcelona)

This bustling urban beach has shallow waters, lifeguards, and a lively promenade with plenty of kid-friendly amenities like ice cream shops and playgrounds.

Llafranc Beach (Costa Brava)

Ideal for families, this beach offers calm, clear waters and soft sand, with nearby restaurants and a quaint seaside village to explore.

Calafell Beach (Costa Daurada)

A wide, sandy stretch with shallow waters perfect for little ones. The seafront is vibrant, with play areas and plenty of room for games.

Tamariu Beach (Costa Brava)

Surrounded by pine-covered hills, this charming beach features tranquil waters perfect for swimming and paddle boarding with kids.

Outdoor Adventures for Kids

Hiking in Montseny Natural Park

This stunning reserve, a UNESCO Biosphere site, has family-friendly trails, picnic spots, and lush forests to explore.

Cycling the Via Verda (Greenways)

Converted railway lines offer safe, flat cycling routes through scenic areas, with popular options near Girona and the Ter River.

Kayaking on the Ebro River

Gentle kayaking tours are a fun way for families to enjoy Catalonia's waterways while spotting local wildlife.

Discovering the Garrotxa Volcanic Zone

This volcanic park is perfect for easy hikes and picnics, offering a glimpse into the region's unique geology.

Dalí Scavenger Hunt in Figueres

Introduce kids to art and culture with a fun scavenger hunt through Salvador Dalí's hometown, finishing at his surreal Theatre-Museum.

Catalonia offers the perfect mix of sandy beaches and outdoor fun to keep kids entertained and engaged.

Interactive Museums and Cultural Experiences for All Ages

Hands-On Museums in Catalonia

CosmoCaixa (Barcelona)

This interactive science museum features engaging exhibits, an indoor rainforest, and a planetarium, making it a hit with both kids and adults.

Catalonia Toy Museum (Figueres)

Explore a delightful collection of toys from various eras. Kids can play with some exhibits, while adults enjoy the nostalgic journey.

Museu Blau (Natural Science Museum, Barcelona)

Fossils, minerals, and interactive displays make this museum a fascinating destination for those curious about Earth's history.

Music Museum (Barcelona)

Discover the history of music through hands-on exhibits, including opportunities to play a variety of instruments.

CaixaForum (Barcelona)

This cultural center offers family-friendly art exhibits, workshops, and creative activities that inspire visitors of all ages.

Memorable Cultural Activities

Castells (Human Towers)

Watch the breathtaking tradition of human tower building at festivals or join a workshop to learn how these towers are created.

Family Cooking Classes

Learn to prepare Catalan classics like paella or panellets in a fun, hands-on cooking class perfect for families.

Poble Espanyol (Barcelona)

Stroll through this replica Spanish village showcasing architecture, crafts, and cultural traditions, complete with workshops for kids.

Local Festivals

Experience vibrant events like La Patum in Berga or Correfocs, where fire, music, and costumes create unforgettable memories.

Chocolate Museum (Barcelona)

This sweet experience includes exhibits on the history of chocolate, tastings, and fun workshops for visitors of all ages.

Catalonia offers a rich variety of interactive museums and cultural activities that provide fun and learning for the whole family.

Planning a Memorable Family Trip

Planning a family trip to Catalonia combines culture, nature, and fun for all ages. Here's how to make it unforgettable:

Barcelona: A City Full of Magic

Top Attractions: Wander through Park Güell and marvel at the Sagrada Família's unique architecture. Explore the Gothic Quarter or stroll along Las Ramblas for a mix of history and entertainment.

Family Activities: Visit CosmoCaixa, an engaging science museum, or L'Aquàrium, famous for its underwater tunnel.

Beach Fun: Head to Barceloneta or Nova Icaria beaches, ideal for kids with their shallow waters and playgrounds.

Costa Brava: Scenic Coasts and Charming Villages

Seaside Getaways: Popular spots like Lloret de Mar and Platja d'Aro offer family-friendly beaches, while Calella de Palafrugell provides a quieter escape.

Cultural Stops: Explore the Dalí Theatre-Museum in Figueres or wander through medieval villages like Pals and Peratallada.

Montserrat: Stunning Views and History

Hop on the scenic train to Montserrat to visit the monastery and enjoy family-friendly hiking trails. Don't miss the boys' choir performances.

PortAventura World: A Theme Park Adventure

Located in Salou, this massive park features thrilling rides, live shows, a water park, and the unique Ferrari Land.

Pyrenees: Outdoor Adventures

Activities: Go hiking, take the rack railway to Núria Valley, or try horseback riding. In winter, family skiing at La Molina is a hit.

Rustic Villages: Explore picturesque towns like Rupit and Beget for a slower-paced experience.

Girona: A Walk Through History

Old Town: Stroll along the medieval walls and spot filming locations from *Game of Thrones*.

Interactive Fun: The Museum of Cinema offers hands-on exhibits perfect for kids.

Family Travel Tips

Getting Around: Use public transport for cities and consider renting a car for rural exploration.

Food: Enjoy sharing tapas or pintxos, with restaurants often catering to young diners.

Stays: Opt for family-oriented hotels or rentals with outdoor spaces and pools.

CHAPTER 10: PRACTICAL INFORMATION AND TRAVEL TIPS

Accommodation: Hotels, Villas, and Rural Retreats

Catalonia offers a wide range of accommodations to suit every family's preferences, whether you're after city convenience, seaside relaxation, or a peaceful countryside retreat.

Hotels: Easy and Comfortable

In Barcelona: Family-friendly options like **Hotel Barcelona Catedral** provide spacious rooms and a central location near top attractions.

On the Costa Brava: Choose beachfront stays like **Hotel Alàbriga & Home Suites** in Sant Feliu de Guíxols, complete with pools and kids' activities.

In Girona: Stay at boutique hotels like **Hotel Nord 1901**, close to the historic center.

Near PortAventura: Themed hotels such as **Hotel Gold River** offer fun and easy access to the theme park.

Villas: Space and Independence

Villas are ideal for families seeking privacy and flexibility.

Costa Brava: Rent a villa with sea views in Begur or Tossa de Mar, often featuring private pools and outdoor terraces.

Countryside Retreats: Rural villas in regions like Empordà provide quiet settings near vineyards and medieval villages.

Barcelona Outskirts: Suburban villas close to train links offer a mix of calm and city access.

Rural Getaways: Peace and Charm

For a slower pace, rural stays combine natural beauty with cozy accommodations.

Masias: Traditional farmhouses, like **Masia Can Cuch** in Montseny Natural Park, offer rustic charm with modern amenities.

Eco-Lodges: Enjoy eco-friendly stays in the Pyrenees, perfect for hiking, biking, or stargazing.

Wine Regions: Stay in Penedès or Priorat to explore vineyards and enjoy family-friendly winery visits.

Unique Experiences

Treehouses: Try **Cabanes als Arbres**, where you can sleep among the treetops for a magical nature escape.

Historic Stays: Experience a night in a castle or monastery, like **Parador de Cardona**, for a touch of history.

Whether you prefer urban sophistication or rural tranquility, Catalonia's accommodations cater to all tastes and family needs.

Language, Currency, and Etiquette

Language

Catalan and Spanish: Both Catalan and Spanish are official languages in Catalonia. Catalan is widely spoken and seen on signs, while Spanish is also universally understood. English is commonly spoken in tourist areas.

Helpful Phrases: Learning a few Catalan phrases like *Hola* (Hello), *Si us plau* (Please), and *Gràcies* (Thank you) can go a long way.

Currency

Euro (€): The euro is the currency used throughout Catalonia. Credit and debit cards are widely accepted, but it's handy to carry some cash for small purchases or when visiting rural areas.

Tipping: Tipping is not obligatory but appreciated. Rounding up or leaving 5-10% in restaurants for good service is common.

Etiquette

Greetings: Handshakes are typical for formal introductions, while friends and family often exchange kisses on both cheeks.

Dining Culture: Meals are enjoyed later, with lunch typically around 2 PM and dinner after 8 PM. Tapas and shared dishes are a big part of the social dining experience.

Dress Code: Casual yet stylish attire is standard, though it's best to dress modestly when visiting churches or religious sites.

Behavior: Be considerate of local customs and avoid being loud or disruptive, particularly in quiet or rural areas.

Local Customs

Sundays and Siestas: Many businesses close on Sundays and for afternoon breaks, usually between 2 and 5 PM.

Cultural Identity: Catalans take pride in their unique heritage. Acknowledging Catalonia as a distinct region rather than just part of Spain is appreciated.

Safety, Health, and Emergency Contacts

Safety

Overall Safety: Catalonia is a generally safe destination, but be cautious of pickpockets in busy areas like Las Ramblas in Barcelona or on crowded public transport. Keep valuables secure and avoid leaving bags unattended.

Driving Tips: Roads are in good condition, but exercise care on winding roads in rural or mountainous areas. Always wear seatbelts and follow local traffic laws.

Health

Medical Services: Catalonia has a high-quality healthcare system. EU citizens can use the European Health Insurance Card (EHIC), while others should ensure they have travel insurance covering medical care.

Pharmacies: Pharmacies (*farmàcies*) are easy to find and can help with minor health issues. A green cross marks them, and 24-hour locations are listed on signage.

Drinking Water: Tap water is safe across Catalonia, but bottled water is also widely available if you prefer.

Emergency Contacts

Universal Emergency Number: Dial **112** for police, fire, or medical emergencies.

Tourist Assistance: In Barcelona, the Tourist Police can be reached at +34 93 484 4848.

Medical Emergencies: Call **061** for non-critical health concerns or medical advice.

Lost Credit Cards: Notify your bank immediately to block the card. Major providers like Visa and Mastercard offer 24/7 global assistance.

Extra Advice

Sun Protection: Use sunscreen, stay hydrated, and avoid peak sun hours during the summer months.

COVID-19 Updates: Check current guidelines on masks and vaccination requirements.

Outdoor Safety: When hiking or exploring, inform someone of your plans, carry essentials like water and snacks, and ensure your phone is fully charged.

Sustainability and Responsible Tourism

Catalonia is dedicated to sustainable tourism, aiming to preserve its natural wonders, cultural heritage, and thriving tourism sector. Here's how visitors can play a part in keeping the region vibrant and well-preserved:

Eco-Friendly Travel Options

Public Transport: Take advantage of Catalonia's comprehensive train, metro, and bus systems to lower your environmental impact. Many destinations, including coastal and nature spots, are easily reachable by train.

Cycling: Cities like Barcelona and Girona offer bike rentals and bike-friendly paths, perfect for exploring sustainably.

Electric Vehicles: If you're driving, consider renting an electric or hybrid car, with plenty of charging stations available across the region.

Sustainable Accommodation

Eco-Certified Hotels: Choose accommodations that hold eco-certifications like Biosphere or EU Ecolabel, which focus on energy conservation and waste management.

Eco-Friendly Stays: Opt for rural stays such as eco-lodges or restored farmhouses (*masias*) that emphasize sustainability and often offer locally grown organic food.

Protecting Natural Areas

National Parks: Respect the environment by staying on marked trails, disposing of trash properly, and observing wildlife in protected areas like Montseny or Aigüestortes.

Beach Conservation: Keep beaches clean by using designated waste bins and avoiding single-use plastic products.

Supporting Local Communities

Eat Local: Support restaurants and markets that serve dishes made with local ingredients from the region.

Shop Local: Buy handcrafted goods from local artisans instead of mass-produced souvenirs.

Cultural Sensitivity: Show respect for local customs and language, such as learning a few words in Catalan, to appreciate the region's identity.

Minimizing Waste

Reusable Products: Bring your own reusable water bottle, shopping bags, and utensils to reduce plastic waste. Tap water is safe, and refill stations are available in many places.

Recycling: Use Catalonia's color-coded bins for recycling (yellow for plastics, blue for paper, green for glass).

Sustainable Activities

Eco-Tours: Choose guided tours that emphasize environmental conservation and explore lesser-known areas to help reduce over-tourism.

Slow Travel: Embrace a slower travel pace to immerse yourself in local culture, avoiding rushed itineraries and enjoying a more meaningful experience.

By making sustainable choices, you'll help protect Catalonia's beauty and support its local communities, ensuring it remains a vibrant destination for future travelers.

Maps and navigation tools

For navigating Catalonia, combining digital and physical tools works best, especially in less connected areas.

Digital Options

Google Maps: Great for city navigation, public transport, and walking routes in places like Barcelona and Girona.

Moovit: Handy for real-time public transport updates in urban areas.

Komoot: Excellent for planning hikes and cycling trips, with detailed routes in Catalonia's natural parks.

AllTrails: Perfect for finding hiking trails in Montserrat, the Pyrenees, or along Costa Brava.

Wikiloc: Popular locally for GPS routes covering hiking, biking, and outdoor adventures.

Paper Maps

IGN (Institut Cartogràfic de Catalunya): Detailed hiking and rural maps, available in bookstores or online.

Michelin Maps: Ideal for planning road trips and scenic drives.

Tourist Office Maps: Free maps highlighting local sights, available from tourist information centers.

Tips

Download offline maps via Google Maps or Maps.me to navigate areas with weak connectivity.

Bring a physical map for hikes in remote spots like the Pyrenees, where mobile signals may drop.

CHAPTER 11: SUGGESTED ITINERARIES

7-Day Journey: Coastal, Cultural, and Rural Explorations

Day 1: Barcelona – A Cultural Icon

Visit landmarks like Sagrada Família and Park Güell.

Wander through the Gothic Quarter and La Rambla.

Wrap up the day with views from Montjuïc or Barceloneta Beach.

Day 2: Costa Brava – Seaside Escapes

Drive to Costa Brava (1.5 hours).

Explore picturesque towns like Calella de Palafrugell and Begur.

Relax at stunning beaches such as Platja de Castell or Aiguablava.

Day 3: Girona – History and Charm

Stroll Girona's medieval streets and cross its famous bridges.

Visit the Cathedral and the Jewish Quarter.

Savor Catalan specialties at a local eatery.

Day 4: Figueres – Dalí's Wonderland

Head to Figueres (30 minutes from Girona).

Explore the Salvador Dalí Theatre-Museum.

Discover nearby villages like Peralada for a laid-back vibe.

Day 5: Montserrat – Nature and Spirituality

Travel to Montserrat (1.5 hours from Barcelona).

Hike scenic trails and visit the monastery.

Take in panoramic views of the rugged mountains.

Day 6: Penedès or Priorat – Wine Regions

Tour vineyards in Penedès for cava or Priorat for robust reds.

Sample wines and enjoy the peaceful countryside.

Stay overnight at a rural inn or farmhouse.

Day 7: Tarragona – Roman History

Discover Tarragona's Roman amphitheater, aqueduct, and historic center.

Unwind on sandy beaches before heading back to Barcelona.

Suggestions

A rental car is ideal for flexibility, especially in rural areas.

Book tickets in advance for popular attractions like Sagrada Família and Montserrat. Don't miss local dishes like escalivada, fideuà, and crema catalana along the journey.

Thematic Routes: Wine, History, and Nature

Wine Route: Penedès and Priorat

Penedès: Visit famous wineries like Codorníu or Freixenet, tour vineyards, learn about cava production, and enjoy tastings.

Priorat: Known for its bold red wines, this region offers charming villages like Gratallops and Porrera, surrounded by dramatic landscapes. Pair wines with dishes like escalivada or pa amb tomàquet.

History Route: Tarragona and Girona

Tarragona: Explore Roman landmarks like the amphitheater and aqueduct, and visit the National Archaeological Museum.

Girona: Walk through the medieval Jewish Quarter, visit the Cathedral, and admire the colorful houses along the Onyar River. Add Besalú to see a beautifully preserved medieval village.

Nature Route: Montserrat and Costa Brava

Montserrat: Hike scenic trails, visit the monastery, and take in panoramic mountain views.

Costa Brava: Enjoy rugged coastlines, turquoise waters, and hidden coves. Walk the Camí de Ronda or snorkel in spots like Begur or Tossa de Mar. Extend to Cap de Creus or Aiguamolls de l'Empordà for more nature.

Tips

Each route can be done in a day or extended. A rental car is recommended for flexibility. Book wine tastings or tours in advance for a richer experience.

Day Trips: Montserrat, Andorra, and the French Pyrenees

Montserrat

Just an hour from Barcelona, Montserrat is ideal for hiking, spiritual visits, and incredible views. Explore the Montserrat Monastery and its Black Madonna, and if you're lucky, hear the boys' choir. For panoramic views, hike the Sant Jeroni trail or take the funicular for easier access.

Andorra

About 2.5 hours from Barcelona, Andorra offers shopping, mountain beauty, and outdoor activities. Visit Andorra la Vella for shopping and spas, or head to Vallnord or Grandvalira for hiking in summer or skiing in winter.

French Pyrenees

A 2–3 hour drive brings you to this scenic region filled with charming villages and stunning mountains. Explore Villefranche-de-Conflent, a UNESCO site, or ride the scenic Yellow Train (Train Jaune). Nature lovers can visit the Pyrenees National Park or hike in Cerdagne.

Tips

Leave early, especially for Andorra and the French Pyrenees, to make the most of your day.

Bring hiking gear if you plan to explore.

Check any border crossing regulations for Andorra and France.

CONCLUSION

Catalonia is a destination brimming with discovery, offering a remarkable mix of history, culture, and stunning landscapes. From the lively streets of Barcelona to the serene mountain villages of the Pyrenees, this region provides a wide range of experiences. Whether you're exploring the coastal beauty of Costa Brava, stepping back in time among Roman ruins in Tarragona, or indulging in world-class wines in Penedès, Catalonia captivates with its diversity and charm. This guide has merely touched upon the many wonders of the area, and no matter where your travels take you, Catalonia promises to create lasting memories. Let it inspire your next adventure, where every corner reveals something extraordinary.

Printed in Great Britain
by Amazon